Praise for *The Power of a Br*

"Healing is about much more than curing, as Julie Interrante vividly shows in this marvelous book. I am reminded of the mythic legend of the wounded healer, who is paradoxically empowered by his own woundedness. So, too, are many patients empowered in the wake of their encounter with health challenges. Thank you, Julie Interrante, for revealing the complexity and wonder of the healing journey."

—Larry Dossey, MD
Author of *The Power of Premonitions*

"*The Power of a Broken-Open Heart* is exactly the power we all need to embrace if we are to live fully. This book will guide you to remember this power."

—Christiane Northrup, MD
Author of *The Secret Pleasures of Menopause*

"In the ceremonial medicine I have studied, we talk about death as the ally— which implies learning to access the wisdom that comes when we remain mindful of our own mortality. Julie Interrante's book shows us just how powerful this wisdom can be and how ordinary people like ourselves can access deep insight and joy by allowing the pain of loss to break our hearts open. *The Power of a Broken-Open Heart* is a moving and authentic account of how to live every moment until you die."

—Oriah Mountain Dreamer
Author of *The Invitation*

"*The Power of a Broken-Open Heart* is a compelling work for our time. Right from the introduction, I knew I was reading something I wanted to understand and be able to articulate. I was surprised to find my own heart mending as I read through the stories and guidance. Here was the gentle support I needed to integrate the pieces my heart had broken into when my father died. I trust this book will do the same and so much more for you."

—Edward Viljoen, DD
Center for Spiritual Living

"A rabbi once observed, 'God so loved stories that he invented people.' The people God invented to share their wisdom in this book will touch your heart. Julie Interrante's honest and gentle invitation to embrace the lessons of these patient-teachers for a happier life today is beautifully woven throughout."

—Rev. Georgia Prescott, Center for Spiritual Awareness

"With grace and humility, Julie Interrante takes the reader to places of the heart where so many are afraid to go. *The Power of a Broken-Open Heart* teaches all of us how to trust, let go, and come to understand that love will guide us through our own ultimate journey."

—Rev. Mark Anthony Lord
Author of *The Seven Living Words*

"Julie Interrante's insights lead us to hold our lives lightly and compassionately, freeing us to trust the divine promise of abundant life."

-Rev. Mary Lynn Tobin
Pastor, Davis Presbyterian Community Church
Davis, California

"I read this book hoping to learn more about dying; instead, I learned more about living. While many of us grow up learning how to hide our emotions, Julie Interrante teaches us how to 'break open our hearts.' This is a book you will want to share with others. A 'must' for library shelves, it offers hope during difficult times."

—Daryl Morrison
Librarian
University of California, Davis

"*The Power of a Broken-Open Heart* is a courageous look at life through the lens of our impermanence. Here Julie Interrante offers us a key to greater wellness—living each day awake to its offerings. Most of all, she offers us herself, alive on every page, her heart and passion shining through every word."

—Susan Frazier, Managing Partner
Smith Flat Center for Health
Placerville, California

"Last summer, I was informed that my son had been killed in Afghanistan. My world disintegrated. The standard self-help books seemed trivial. In this book, hospice worker and scholar Julie Interrante masterfully tackles the all-too-often neglected and forbidden subjects of death, darkness, and disintegration. She capably demonstrates that all of the 'seasons of life' are normal and necessary for a complete spiritual experience. Read this book!"

—Michael Bogar, MDiv, ThM
Spiritual Enrichment Center of Bainbridge Island,
Washington

The Power of a
BROKEN-OPEN HEART

May I speak the words that silence has never spoken
May I sing the melody of a heart that's broken open
And may we all know this peace that's everlasting,
And may we all sing, hallelujah.

The Power of a
BROKEN-OPEN HEART

Life-Affirming Wisdom from the Dying

JULIE INTERRANTE, MA

WITH A FOREWORD BY
HUGH PRATHER

Compassionate Arts
PUBLISHING
ALBUQUERQUE, NEW MEXICO

Published by:

COMPASSIONATE ARTS PUBLISHING
PO Box 35466
Albuquerque, NM 87176

Editing: Ellen Kleiner
Book design and production: Angela Werneke
Cover and flute art: Cari Pier
Graphics illustration: Felicia Montoya
Author photo: Susan Lawton

Copyright © 2009 by Julie Interrante

The Power of a Broken-Open Heart is factually accurate, except that names, locales, and individual traits have been altered to preserve coherence while protecting privacy.

Printed in the United States of America

PUBLISHER'S CATALOGING-IN-PUBLICATION DATA

Interrante, Julie.
The power of a broken- open heart : life-affirming wisdom from the
dying / Julie Interrante. -- 1st ed. -- Albuquerque, NM :
Compassionate Arts Publishing, c2009.

    p. ; cm.

ISBN: 9780984095605
Running title: Broken-open heart.
Includes bibliographical references.

    1. Life change events-- Psychological aspects. 2. Conduct of life.
3. Stress (Psychology) 4. Terminally ill -- Psychology. I. Title.
II. Title: Broken-open heart.

BF637.L53 I58 2009   2009930022
155.9/3-- dc22   0911

10 9 8 7 6 5 4 3 2 1

To all the people
I've worked with over the years
who shared their journeys with me
and
in memory of my father,
Fred (Fritz) Kuebelbeck,
who taught me the value of seeking

My deepest gratitude to . . .

My mother, Lillian, for being a pillar of strength and prayer;

My sisters—Jan, Victoria, and Michele—for our bond, the foundation on which I stand every day;

My husband, Ross, for his inexhaustible love and kindness and for encouraging me every step of the way;

My heart companion, Michelle, without whom this book would not exist, for her endless hours of working with me, feeding me, tucking me in, and unconditionally loving me;

My closest friend, mentor, and soul companion, Georgia, for always pointing me in the right direction, holding my feet to the fire, and loving me unconditionally;

My dear friend Jean, for walking with Ross and me through open-heart surgery and loving us no matter what;

My colleague and heart friend Jeremy, for standing with me in the big questions, telling the truth, and making suggestions on the manuscript;

My companions on the path, Susan and Dave, for saving me in the midst of breaking open and giving me an experience of unconditional openheartedness;

My dogs, Maggie and Daisy, for making me laugh and get outside every day;

Maria Henson, for kicking it all off in an interview, taking risks, and living full out;

My friend and pedicure partner, Angela, for all her support;

My friend Robert, for recognizing our deep connection without regard to time;

Linus, who encouraged the publishing of this book long before I could imagine it;

Everyone at Blessingway—Ellen, Angela, and Karen—whose creativity and skills have transformed this book;

My friend and artist Cari, for her love of beauty and for loving this project; and

My chaplaincy students, for clarifying the teachings and for laughing and loving while learning.

Grateful acknowledgment is also made for permission to reprint "The Circles of Life" from *Many Winters* by Nancy Wood and "The Unbroken" from *Beyond Brokenness* by Rashani Réa.

Contents

Foreword: The Place Inside

My dad will soon be ninety-nine. For some time, he has been under hospice care in his home, where he prefers to stay, gently refusing any benefit that might come from a hospital visit.

What I find remarkable about this stage of his life is that although his body is swiftly disintegrating (his teeth are falling out, his hearing is almost gone, his eyesight is bad, he has little ability to recall nouns, he has to wear diapers, and he spends his day either in a wheelchair or in bed) he is nevertheless in good spirits most of the time. In fact, he even jokes about what is happening to his body:

"How are you feeling, Dad?"

"Not as good as when I was ninety-six."

"Are you still enjoying life?"

"Well, I'm down to just one girlfriend."

Here is a man who was bigger, stronger, and

better looking than most, a good athlete who loved adventure, enjoyed excellent health, and was always active. Each of these things, as well as every one of his friends, has been taken from him. All he has left is the lightheartedness he has had for as long as I have known him.

The way my dad achieved release from the physical tragedy of age and accident is fairly straightforward. After several bouts with himself over whether he wanted to die or live to be one hundred, he realized he had no control over that—and wanted no control. He came to peace with both living *and* dying. In other words, he took himself off the battlefield. Bypassing the conflict over whether to live or die, he leaned back into his life as it was. This allowed him to regain his basic happiness, and now he is neither waiting for the inevitable nor fighting to stave it off.

What is the key to my father's state of mind, or any peaceful state of mind? Julie Interrante answers this question in many unique ways in her short masterpiece *The Power of a Broken-Open Heart*.

One thought that particularly struck me was, "If dying is not about the body, it follows that life is not about the body" (p. 114).

I cannot state what I believe to be the answer as eloquently or incisively as Julie has in this book, but I will try: The purpose of the mind is not to serve the body. Therefore, do whatever allows your body to be less of a preoccupation. As best you can and only within the moment at hand, release your mind. Resign as its instructor. Resign as its judge and jury. It already knows the way to "the place inside which is unbreakable and whole" (Rashani Réa, p. 107). Make a leap of faith and release your mind, and it will take you home.

Obviously it is easier to give voice to this concept than to put it into practice, which is why I am so grateful Julie has written this book. Even if it contained nothing else, the intimate accounts of people with whom she has worked are helpful beyond measure. Anyone in need who picks up this book will find that at least one person's story reflects their own.

But that isn't all they will receive. They will feel an almost motherly love engulf them as Julie shares her heart with the reader. It is as if she knows us personally, intimately. She opens our hearts and pours in comfort.

Hugh Prather

Introduction

Although this book is rooted in wisdom from the dying, it is not a book about dying but about living more consciously having accepted mortality as a natural transition. During my years as a hospital and hospice chaplain, I was amazed at how many people felt caught off guard when they realized they were dying. I believe this is because most people have not consciously walked through the many changes in their lives that are the practice ground for the transition of dying. Similarly, during the many memorial services I have led, I have often heard people comment on the unexpected nature of death and lament the deceased person's short time on earth. What is regrettable for many people facing death, however, is not so much the lack of time they have on earth but the lack of *quality* time. If we can embrace the fact that we will die someday, we will live more fully in the present.

I'll never forget José, a ninety-three-year-old man who, when I visited him for the first time, looked at me with tears in his eyes and said: "It's too soon. I'm not supposed to die yet. I have more to do. I have to get better and go back to my ranch. I pray to God every day to heal me."

While touched by his tenacity and faith, I wanted to say, "But José, you're ninety-three years old!" I wanted to explain to him that our culture has not helped us comprehend the power and inevitability of life's changes. Instead, I listened to José paint a picture of the life he was not ready to leave, describing his ranch, horses, wife, and children; the things he had loved and lost; and the hard work he had done to a small piece of ground he called his ranch. I wondered if when I was ninety-three I would resist death, like José, calling out to the gods to heal me, or whether I would welcome the transition that death brings.

José and others have taught me a great deal about life—that our acceptance of death has nothing to do with the number of years we have walked the planet but with how fully we have lived. I have stood next to a grieving mother as she held her dying three-year-old, witnessing her moment of transition from grasping to release. I have seen spouses, partners, and siblings angry one moment and weeping the next as they struggled with disconnecting life support. I have heard people nearing death describe the heaven they see and been privy to conversations between the dying and the already dead. I have listened to the elderly recount life events with joy yet harbor regrets about things not done. Such encounters have taught me that I don't want to come to the end of my life feeling I didn't live the way I had hoped to, that I'd played it safe rather than living fully.

I understand the resistance to facing death when there is so much living to be done, but the truth is it is on our minds nevertheless, even if unconsciously. Fear of death is the basis of all other fears. Every time we fear losing money or losing someone we love, any time we become resistant to something or controlling, we are actually experiencing the fear of dying. As Buddhists maintain, we can use life events to practice for the moment of death, allowing experiences to remind us that nothing is permanent and that even in impermanence everything is perfect.

Working with the dying has shown me that it is time to talk about dying. By remaining quiet about it, we are allowing ourselves, our culture, and our world to act out our fear—to fight and hurt and kill in an attempt to convince ourselves that we have control over death. Accepting, and even embracing, the idea that we are impermanent beings brings a freedom to live more from our hearts and gives us the courage to take risks in order to live a full, unapologetic life. When we consciously observe our transitions and accept that everything changes, we have greater peace of mind and presence of heart to live life with more awareness and joy.

CHAPTER ONE

Breaking Open

When I rise up
let me rise up joyful like a bird.
When I fall
let me fall without regret like a leaf.

–Wendell Berry

Although most of us try to avoid fully experiencing pain, it has many benefits. For one thing, it breaks open the heart so that emotional movement can occur, something I experienced in a moment of despair one stormy afternoon.

It was raining inside my heart as hard as it was raining outside my car. I screamed to the universe, "I can't do this anymore! If you want me to con-

tinue working with the dying, send me a sign. I've got to know I'm not all alone out here!" I sat a long time staring out my windshield, my vision blurred from the tears and the rain, my energy spent from my immersion in fear, loneliness, and despair.

Then, trying to pull myself together so I could lead Jackie's memorial service, I scolded myself, "Okay, girl, you don't get to do this right now. Those people need you."

Grabbing my flute, I ran into the community building of Jackie's apartment complex. Her partner, Kate, met me at the door, looking anxious. "I'm glad you're here," she said, relieved. "I don't know how this is going to go."

Jackie, a forty-two-year-old woman who died of colon cancer the week before, had been certain she would beat her cancer and ride her Harley again, but she didn't. Her gorgeous turquoise motorcycle stood outside the door in tribute to her spirit and tenacity.

By the time we were ready to start the memorial service, the room was packed with family and friends. As always, I began by closing my eyes, praying, and playing my flute, feeling particularly grateful this night for the instrument's power to center me.

As I finished, the front door opened, and in walked a man with long black hair and olive skin. Behind him came a woman with a soft complexion and long curly red hair, carrying a baby about a year old. Suddenly, my heart leapt toward the gentleman, certain we had met before. Although distracted, I ended the service by asking everyone to recite a Buddhist blessing.

People began to talk and mingle. Then, as if the Red Sea had parted, the gentleman I thought I had recognized came to me with his hand out and said, "That was a most wonderful service. Nice to make your acquaintance. This is my wife and my son."

I shook his hand, saying, "You seem so familiar to me. I am certain we've met. Did I meet you at Jackie's?"

"No," he replied, holding my hand.

"I'm just certain I know you," I insisted.

Then, leaning toward me and giving me a gentle hug, he said into my ear, "That's because I knew you before we got here."

Electricity shot up my spine. He looked at me momentarily with gentle eyes, then left. I drove home in the rain wondering if my call for help had been answered.

The week following Jackie's memorial service I was the emcee at a Christmas celebration honoring individuals who had died in our local hospice that year. As we were beginning the program, an elderly gentleman, holding the hand of a woman who appeared to be his wife, walked from the back row of chairs up to the front looking for a place to sit. He seemed familiar, and I thought that someone he loved must have been in hospice and I'd been to see them.

After a candle lighting and closing song, I thanked everyone for participating and invited them inside for cookies and coffee. The gentleman shook my hand and thanked me for the lovely service. "Do I know you?" I asked. "Have I worked with you, or been to your home?"

"Oh, no! I'm certain you haven't," he said, grinning.

"What's your name? I asked.

Looking uncomfortable, as if caught unawares, he replied, "Um—my name's Smith."

"You seem familiar to me," I insisted.

Then, leaning forward and giving me a hug, he said into my ear, "That's because I knew you before we got here."

I felt my knees buckle and every hair on my body stand on end. I took his hand and said, my voice a little unsteady, "You are the second person in three days who has said that to me."

He smiled softly and replied, "I know."

I was speechless as he led his wife into the building to join the others. I greeted the remaining families in line, but all I could think about was getting inside and finding the man and his companion to discover their identities. When I searched for the couple, however, I could not find them. Although I was disappointed at not learning more about them, I knew they had delivered their message: I had received the help I urgently sought, a sign that I was not alone.

Working with people who are sick and dying has given me the opportunity to witness the benefits of surrender and see that suffering can catalyze personal transformation. Sometimes their transformation has come through actually dying, while other times it has come through sorrow that has permitted them to connect with family, friends, and themselves in a new way. No one taught me the power of surrender more than Luann, a fifty-six-year-old woman who desperately wanted to die.

Luann had just been admitted into our hospice program. She was in excruciating pain, and nothing we were doing for her medically was working. When I walked into her smoke-filled home, she was lying in a hospital bed in the center of the living room.

"I hope you don't mind that I smoke," she muttered.

"Hi, my name is Julie," I choked. "It's nice to meet you."

I recognized the signs of dying. Luann was bone thin. She was struggling for breath and angry. "I am done. I want out," she said. "I have such horrible pain, I can't lie still. It's been like this for weeks. I hope you can do something to help me. No one else has been able to."

"I play the Native American flute. How about if I play for you?" I asked.

"I would like that," she replied.

I played my flute, and when I was finished she said, "Okay, that's all I need. You can go now. Thank you for coming."

I agreed to return in a week, wondering if she would die before that. In fact, I visited Luann weekly for the next eight weeks, marveling at how tenaciously she hung on to life while saying she was ready to die.

During another visit, Luann made it clear she

believed in a power greater than herself and was mad at that power because she was suffering. She said the only thing that really brought her any comfort was the sound of the flute. As I removed my flute from its case, Luann pointed at the garage, outside the window, revealing matter-of-factly, "My thirty-two-year-old son committed suicide in that garage. I'm sick of the pain, and I want to die. Julie, what is taking so long? Can you help me die?"

"I don't know," I said. "Are you mad at your son for taking his life?"

"Oh, no! I love him no matter what," she replied emphatically.

Wondering if that could be true, I asked, "Have you been able to forgive him?"

"Oh, yeah! Now play your flute," she ordered.

As the sound of my flute filled the room, I heard a quiet noise like that of a baby uttering its first sound. Then Luann turned her face toward the heavens and howled to the universe, "I am so sorry, Craig, I didn't know." Luann's emaciated body convulsed with sobs. I sat in awe, witnessing her experience of pain as she delivered the message of her broken-open heart.

When she quieted, I put my flute back in its case. Knowing there was nothing more to say, I leaned over the bed and gave her a hug.

"Thank you," she whispered.

As I got into my car, I was aware that I had seen a sacred transformation brought on by Luann's embrace of her pain, and I was not surprised when two days later she died.

Luann taught me the value of consciously facing pain, how surrendering to it can bring about personal transformation. Allowing our hearts to break open transforms everything—our perspective on life, our ability to connect with other people, our capacity to live life to the fullest, and our willingness to accept death as a necessary transition in the life cycle.

CHAPTER TWO

The Broken-Open Heart

Sadness flowers
to the next renewing joy.

—Gareb Teague

If the broken-open heart can transform us, why do we resist the experience of pain and heartbreak? I believe it is because we have convinced ourselves that pain means something is wrong. Indeed, we have made an unconscious agreement to avoid pain at all cost. We have created a culture bent on numbing it—through substance abuse, eating, and shopping, for instance—rather than experiencing it and allowing it to transform us.

Being transformed through the broken-open heart is a natural part of the human experience. In fact, it is our initial experience of life. From the time we are conceived, we are nurtured in the comfort of a dark, warm womb connected to the rhythm of our mother's heartbeat. And yet, at some point, the forward movement of life urges us out of the womb, bringing discomfort and finally emergence into the cold, light, noisy environment of the world. If at this time a newborn could talk, she might say, "Something's going wrong here! I was warm, comfortable, and fed. Now I'm squished, cold, and afraid. What is happening to me?"

Yet once we're born we fall in love with being here. This place becomes our home, and we do not want to leave it. So, if tomorrow someone came to us from the other side of the veil and said, "Come on, we love you and we're ready for you," most of us would say, "No thank you. I'm warm. I'm comfortable. I'm fed. I love it here. Not now."

Each of us has survived the birth process and thus the pain of a broken-open heart, and eventually each of us will have to face death, which, like birth, requires that we release how we have known ourselves. In fact, our entire life is a series of transitions that have the potential to break open our hearts.

The natural cycle of life necessitates that as we physically grow we let go of childhood, adolescence, adulthood, and, eventually, life as we know it. Life experiences, such as leaving home, getting jobs, having families, and following the desires of the heart, keep us actively participating in the cycle of life. As such, every time we must let go of something or someone we love, we have the opportunity to embrace pain, rather than run from it, and thus allow it to transform us. Just as an acorn has to break open for an oak tree to grow and spread its magnificent canopy, we, too, must break open so the brilliance of our hearts may be shared. Even when life catches us unprepared with unexpected change, if we allow our hearts to break open we can appreciate life for what it brings rather than for what it is asking us to release. The experience of a broken-open heart brings vulnerability but also perspective and joy, insights I gleaned while spending an afternoon with a gentleman named Archie.

I sat at my desk wondering how I was going to make it through the afternoon as my energy was low. The enormous need at the hospital where I worked felt overwhelming; unable to tell if anything I was doing made a difference, I felt like my efforts were futile. Suddenly, I was jolted out of my looming despair by the sound of the telephone.

"Hello," I answered.

"Hi, I'm glad I found you," a gentleman replied cheerfully.

"Who is this?" I asked.

"Ma'am, this is Archie Baldwin. I'm in room 604 and I'm going home today, but I need a little help before I leave. I want to make a thank-you card for the nurses, but I became blind on Christmas. Do you think you can help me?"

"Sure," I answered, my heart swelling on hearing this man with such delightful energy. "Perhaps he is the miracle I needed to convince myself to show up one more day in this pit of a hospital," I thought. Armed with paper, pens, tape, and a little chocolate from the stash on my desk, I arrived at room 604 to find Archie laying in his bed, knees up, his gown having fallen off them, revealing his diminishing buttocks and scrotum.

"Hi, Archie, I'm Julie, the person you talked with a few minutes ago," I announced. His exposure made me wonder if I should tell him his family jewels were on display or just let it be.

"Thank you for coming," he said. "I really want to make this card. I've received such good care, and I am very grateful."

"How long have you been here?" I asked.

"Since Christmas—that's when I became blind. I was born with one bad eye, but on Christmas I had an aneurysm and now the other one's gone. Even so, I see some things, like the red dots on the ceiling."

I looked at the white ceiling, hoping to see red dots. "Archie, there are no red dots on the ceiling," I replied.

"Well, I see them," he chuckled. "I also saw squirrels playing in the trees this morning. They were chasing each other and having so much fun. I know you can't see them, but I'm quite an outdoorsman. I think that's why I'm seeing squirrels and trees. It's my brain showing me things. I can see things I couldn't see before because my eyes were in the way."

My heart leapt toward this person, who, despite his condition, had a wonderful perspective on life. "Archie," I confided, "I've often wondered, if I had to lose one of my senses would I choose sight. I have suspected it would keep me from making a lot of judgments I base on appearances."

Archie continued, "Yeah. I used to be shy—until Christmas, when I couldn't hold back because of what people looked like. The loss of my sight has made me feel how people are by how they behave, not how they look."

I was amazed that he could see positive aspects of his condition and how these had caused him to let go of old ways.

"Do you remember Walnettos?" he added, smiling.

"Of course I do," I answered, recalling the chewy candies of my youth and the feelings of comfort and joy associated with eating them. The word flooded me with memories of walking to our neighborhood grocery to buy the penny candy.

"Well, I have a whole bag of them over there on the dresser. Get them."

"Just a minute, Archie. Do you like chocolate?"

"Yes, I love it!" he exclaimed.

"Well, I've got some for you in my bag," I told him, glad that I had followed my intuition to bring chocolate along so I had something to share with him.

After he had unwrapped the shiny gold foil from the midnight chocolate, Archie said, "I play the harmonica. It's here somewhere on the bed."

I spotted a black case and handed it to him.

"I haven't played for thirty years," he said, "but here goes."

As he played, I envisioned myself clogging—western tap dancing—but thought better of it after wondering if my blind friend might be startled. Instead, I applauded, and Archie bowed his thanks.

"You really can play," I said admiringly.

"I'm a little rusty, but they used to pay two hundred and forty dollars for me to play!" he explained, smiling at the memory of bygone days.

"So what would you like the card to say?" I asked, bringing us back to the task at hand.

"I just want them to know how good they—and you—have made me feel. It's like I've made new friends for life," he mumbled.

"I think you're wonderful, Archie," I replied.

"Are you a certain religion?" he questioned.

"Not really," I answered. "I like parts of all kinds of traditions."

"I was raised Episcopalian but hated the dogma," he confessed.

"Yeah, dogma is bullshit," I replied.

"You're more beautiful than I thought," he said, laughing and shaking his head back and forth.

We finished the card together, with me drawing purple hearts and writing in red letters a message to all those who had been so kind to him.

"If you'll help me walk to the front desk, I can deliver this myself," he then suggested.

"I'm game if you are, Archie," I agreed.

A nurse at the station frowned at our two-person caravan and asked, "What are you doing?"

"We're delivering a card," I chirped.

"No, with that," she grumbled pointing to the floor.

I turned and saw Archie's catheter bag dragging along behind us and told Archie about her objection.

"Oh, well, think of it as just a little gift for everyone," he said as we laughed.

After we had delivered the card and giggled our way back to his room, I said, "I play the flute. Would you like to hear it?"

"Oh, yes!" he answered.

As I played, Archie's heart broke open and he sobbed. "It's been a long time since I've been touched that deeply," he whispered.

I hugged him and said, "Thank you, Archie, for inviting me to come today."

"Thank you," he replied. "You saved me today."

As I left the room, I thought to myself, "No, you saved me."

Upon reflection, I realized it was my despair that had allowed me to fully experience Archie, while his blindness had been the catalyst for him to really see me. As a result, each of our hearts had broken open spontaneously, moment to moment, in sadness and in joy. Our interaction had led to a joining of souls. I had ceased feeling futile as I helped him express gratitude to others. Imagining what the world would be like if I stopped using my eyes to make judgments, and instead assessed people and situations with only my heart, had dissipated my despondency. For both of us it had been like discovering an oasis in the middle of a desert, a place of hope for him in his blindness and for me in my despair. Because of this, I understood that a broken-open heart is not only about sadness but also about vulnerability, gratitude, and joy.

CHAPTER THREE

Life Is Not What We Think

*Let not your hearts
be troubled,
neither let them be afraid.*

—John 14:27

When we allow our hearts to break open in response to the experiences of life, we see with new eyes—the eyes of the heart. I first learned about the heart's vision from a Vietnam veteran named Al.

The day I met Al, it was rainy and cold, and I was lost. After several phone calls for directions, I finally located his trailer home. By the time I

parked and walked the two blocks to the front door, I was wet and a little cranky.

"So you're the chaplain?" Al asked when I entered. "I expected a holy-type person. This kind of messes with my head," he added as he took a swallow from his glass, which I would later discover contained a supply of rum and Coke to wet his whistle.

Al was a fifty-two-year-old who had flown gunboats at the height of the Vietnam War. As a young army man, he had been fit, cocky, and self-assured, as reflected in the photos he showed me. He had been shot down three times, the last time losing his most beloved companion, a German shepherd.

His eyes filled with tears as he told me how hard he had cried the day he and his dog had been shot out of the sky. He had been captured, eventually spending three months as a prisoner of war in a bamboo cage in a swamp. Now he was dying of liver disease.

Al was impatient, rough, and made no apologies for it. He knew he drank too much and yelled too often at his wife of twenty-five years, who loved him nevertheless. Al used the "F" word so many times in our first thirty minutes together that I finally responded with, "Isn't that f-ing amazing?" in response to a story about his four Chihuahuas. He laughed so loud he scared them into the bedroom before telling me, "You're okay."

At the end of our first visit, he confessed, "I like you. You can come back."

I got up to leave, and all four Chihuahuas barked me out the door as Al's raspy voice reprimanded his furry pals.

I visited Al often, having fallen for him in a most tender way. It was as if he and I had known each other before. Or perhaps I admired the way he expressed his coarse, angry parts without apology, as I'd been masking mine most of my life. Even though he sometimes felt bad about his behavior, he didn't really want to change, and his wife and children loved him just that way.

During later visits, Al began to ask questions

about God and heaven, at times wondering if he was good enough to be in "God's favor." "It bothers me that I killed people," he said, "especially innocent people. I didn't want to or even mean to sometimes, but I did. I wonder if I can be forgiven for that."

"However God works, I don't think there is judgment in death," I replied.

"Really?" Al asked, sounding hopeful.

"Here's how I think about it. You know how much you love your children? Like they could never do anything that would cause you to stop loving them?" I asked.

"I might be plenty pissed at them, but I'd love them always," he replied in earnest.

"Well," what makes us think we could ever do anything that would cause God to stop loving us?" I added.

"I never thought about it like that. Maybe God knows how hard the war was and how sorry I am about having killed people," he said, his lip quivering. He steadied himself with a few swallows of his cocktail and then hollered to his wife, "Ruth, bring me some more."

Ruth was already on her way with a fresh rum and Coke. "You can stay in here and talk with us," Al offered. Ruth declined, saying she was fine in the kitchen. I could tell by her red eyes and nose that she could hear plenty well from there.

"I lost a daughter last year," Al said. "Seven months ago she ran off the road down the levy and drowned. She was such a good person. I love her a lot. A couple of nights ago, I saw her real clear in a dream. I was certain she was alive."

"I'm really sorry, Al," I replied.

"You're a good woman," he responded.

He and I sat side by side on the couch during every visit. Sometimes he would fall asleep during our conversations and end up with his head on my shoulder.

Al continued to teach me how to view things in ways I never expected, while I subtly encouraged him to break open his heart. One day he insisted that we watch his favorite comedy video, which was about four men dressed in flannel shirts who fished, swore, and degraded women. Al howled at their jokes, while I kept saying, "This is disgusting." He responded by telling me to lighten up. Clearly, Al and I did not have the same sense of humor, but his total enjoyment of the video made it enjoyable for me.

One afternoon Al gifted me with two cartoons he had drawn. One was a caricature of himself as the Spam Carving King. He had won the contest eight years in a row. "Spam carving is an art," he said, "and I'm the best! I'm just sorry I'll miss this year's contest. I don't think I'll be here for it," he confessed.

He died quietly two days later, surrounded by his dogs, family, and friends.

I learned from Al that I could care deeply about someone who viewed life very differently from me. I also learned that even a defended person has moments of tenderness when they can be transformed. Although Al appeared to act tough and suppress his feelings, he allowed the pain of dying to break open his heart, making him feel safe enough to cry, laugh, connect with others, and let go.

Like Al, many people approaching death lose their desire to be defensive and instead willingly let their hearts break open for the sake of connecting with people. We can, however, let our hearts break open *all* the time so we feel greater bonds with others and a stronger link to our authentic selves, especially if we keep our mortality in mind. Tibetans say there are two truths in life: one is that we will die, and the other is that we don't know when. Even though we don't know when we will die, realizing that we will die someday helps us live life more fully in the present.

We don't have to wait until we're told we're dying to let life break open our hearts because the truth is we are already dying. From the moment we are born, the natural cycle of life moves us toward our death. Even if we live to be ninety-five, we are here for only a short time.

I recall hearing Buddhist author Jack Kornfield

say, "the trouble is you think you have time." Believing we have time encourages us to remain unconscious of our impermanence—and thus live superficially. A decision to live in our vulnerability, however, changes our experience of life. Therefore, it is important to allow our hearts to break open so we become more conscious of the impermanence of everything, including ourselves, gain a broader perspective on life, and become continuously transformed by our experiences.

CHAPTER FOUR

The Cycle of Seasons

Earth, ourselves, breathe and Awaken.
leaves are Stirring, all Things Moving,
new day Coming, life Renewing.

—Pawnee Prayer

I like the sound of breathing, even as it slows down and stops when the life force leaves the body. The sounds that accompany dying are reverberations of cracking open into expanded life. Such a transformation can be sad and sometimes painful, but it can be equally exhilarating, full of expectation, and joyful, as a faith-led teacher named Mabel showed me.

When I knocked on Mabel's front door for the first time, I heard a faint voice call, "Come on in." I followed her voice through the house to find her in bed, tucked in by a pink comforter. On her nightstand, alongside a tall lamp with a lacy shade, was a plate with half-eaten toast and a half-full cup of tea.

"I'm just finishing my breakfast. My daughter left it for me. She's gone to work but will be back later. I'm so glad you've come," she said.

Mabel, raised in the Deep South, was a devout Baptist who had practiced her faith all her life and was excited about going "home" to God. This was not the excitement of receiving a new bicycle as a child or the thrill of marriage and love. It was a calm, certain excitement.

"I am the head teacher at my church," Mabel said. "Why, just last Sunday I taught the children about Jesus."

I wondered if this could be true given the current state of her health. But then she got up, sat in a lovely chair with a needlepoint cushion, and easily finished her toast and tea while she told me more about her job at church. "It means everything to me to teach those children. I've been doing it so long I don't know what they'll do without me. But I know God will provide," she added.

"Are you ready to die?" I asked.

"Oh, Sugar, I am ready as soon as the Lord is ready to take me. I've seen God, and I can't wait to go home," she crooned. "I read the Bible every day, and it tells me there is a season for everything—a time to be born, a time to die, a time to plant, and a time to reap. This is just my time to die. It's all in the plan. In the meantime, though, I'll be at church teaching those children, singing, and praising the Lord!" It was clear that Mabel lived in service and love and trusted her God and the cycle of life.

Filled with awe at the calm confidence and conviction of this petite, dark woman sitting in her lacy bedroom, I thought, "She should be doing my job instead of me." This woman was both teaching me and healing parts of me that railed against fundamentalist Christianity, whose followers had judged me.

I wondered what I could possibly offer this faith-filled warrior. "Is there anything I can do for you?" I asked.

"Could you pray with me?" she replied.

"Certainly," I said, even though I was apprehensive about whether my prayers would be strong enough to meet the expectations of this courageous woman who had touched my heart.

I prayed the only way I knew how, from the place in my soul that had been opened by my connection to this devout woman.

When I finished, Mabel looked straight into my eyes and, with tears streaming down her cheeks, whispered, "That was lovely. Thank you, dear."

We sat momentarily in the holy space created by the breaking open of our hearts. And it was from the place of her open, faithful heart that, several weeks later, Mabel "went home."

When I think about the scripture to which Mabel referred, I am reminded that the power of life that moves the cycle of seasons, whether in nature or in us, is the same power that she called Jesus and others call Mother Nature, Allah, Great Mystery, or God.

Each of us individually, as well as collectively in our families and communities, is living the same process as nature—the cycle of seasons. My trust in this process was strengthened by an experience I had with Carlos, a forty-five-year-old man dying from pancreatic cancer.

Carlos was being cared for in his mother's home, with his entire family present. I sat on the bed next to him, and he immediately asked, "How do I die, Julie? I have seen where I'm going. It is a beautiful place. Whenever I'm there, I want to stay, and yet somehow I always end up back here. How do I go there and stay?"

"I don't know the answer to that," I replied. "It seems that we actively participate in our dying, just as we actively participate in living. So you can intentionally prepare yourself for dying and moving to the place you have visited," I offered. I then suggested he begin by saying good-bye to all the people he loved. Having recently experienced a painful divorce and its accompanying losses, I realized that, in fact, both Carlos and I were facing a transition and needed to let go to move on. Not only did he need to say good-bye, but so did I.

Carlos replied, "I will do whatever it takes. I am ready to let go." He added that the hardest part for him would be saying good-bye to his mother. He explained that his father had died just two years earlier, and as the new patriarch of the family he felt he would be letting his family down by dying. But Carlos agreed to begin saying good-bye to his mother, as well as to his brothers, sisters, cousins, nephews, and nieces, even if it was painful.

When I returned the following week, Carlos proclaimed, with an air of accomplishment, that he had said good-bye to everyone. "So why am I still here?" he asked, disappointedly.

"All we can do is our part," I said. I asked if there was anything or anyone he thought he was still holding on to.

He replied, "No, I want to go to that beautiful place and stay."

"Then perhaps you just need to wait on God," I replied, sharing with him my belief that there is a time for all things, including death.

I had two more visits with Carlos, during which he again expressed his frustration with waiting to die. During my final visit, as I witnessed Carlos release his last breath to go to his beautiful place, I realized, with more clarity than ever before, that the transition we call death is essentially the same transition we go through every time we experience change in our lives, whether it involves a new job, relationship, or perspective on life.

There is a pattern of life evident in all transitions that is reminiscent of the cycle of seasons. The cycle of seasons reflects the impermanence of our nature. As the Vietnamese Zen Buddhist monk

Thich Nhat Hanh says: "Impermanence means that everything changes and that nothing remains the same in any consecutive moments. And although things change every moment, they still cannot be accurately described as the same or as different from what they were a moment ago."[1]

One way I appreciate and acknowledge the personal cycle of seasons is by watching its reflection in nature. For example, I observe the changes of a favorite tree in my backyard, a Rose of Sharon. All summer it has beautiful purple blossoms with red centers that attract delightful hummingbirds. Every fall as the blossoms drop and the leaves turn yellow, I feel sad that the beauty of the tree is fading, and I witness what appears to be death. As winter comes, and the tree stands bleakly without leaves, I wonder if it will survive the cold or whether I have accidentally killed it. But then as spring arrives, I notice brilliant green sprigs on the branches and sigh with relief that the tree is showing signs of life again, although I still wonder if it will actually bloom once more. As the familiar purple blossoms with red centers reappear, however, I once again trust this new life. Every season, the Rose of Sharon shows me the beauty and balance of the cycle of seasons, inviting me to trust my own natural cycle.

The diagram in figure 4.1 shows the cycle of seasons both in nature and in people. Each season is divided into two parts—early and transitional. The emotions listed in each part are a guideline to what may be felt by an individual at any given time during the cycle.

While the journey through our personal cycle of seasons does not necessarily coincide with nature's cycle of seasons, there may be times when we are in tune with Mother Nature. In addition, nature's cycle of seasons and our personal cycle of seasons serve a similar purpose—deepening and expansion. Just as the seasons in nature's cycle meld into each other, so do the seasons of our lives. What propels us from one personal season to the next is the ebb and flow of our emotions, which can be affected by our external or internal circumstances and can change from moment to moment in their depth and complexity. They may never feel exactly the same twice, and so we may sometimes find it difficult to see them as reflecting specific seasons. For this reason, it is helpful to gain increased awareness of the potential meaning of their nuances by referring to figure 4.2. It is also important to understand that the tempo of their progression can vary; that at times we can complete an entire cycle of seasons within a moment, a day, or a week, while at other times this process can take months or years. We can also fluctuate back and forth between two seasons before moving definitively to the next one.

The beauty of the cycle of seasons is that by allowing ourselves to be fully present in one season, we will, by the transformational power of life itself, whether we are aware of it or not, be moved into the next season and continue to follow the rotation of life. With time and conscious awareness, we learn to trust the wisdom of our cycle of seasons regardless of our expectations or the appearance of things.

To fully understand this model, it is important to look at each season individually and how it relates to the others in the cycle of life. Fall is the planting season, when plants and trees end their productive cycle and their seeds fall to the ground. In this letting go—when the wind scatters the skeletons of dandelions, for example—plants perpetuate life. With fall comes the anticipation of future growth. If we want tulips in the spring, we have to plant bulbs in the fall.

Fall is also the time of planting seeds in anticipation of personal change. During this season we may have feelings of impending transition, such as expectation, uncertainty, agitation, impatience, lethargy, and irritability. Although we may not know what these feelings concern, in the quiet of our hearts the seeds of change are being planted.

What the feelings are is less important than the act of experiencing them, as they are part of breaking open the heart in preparation for change, the vibrational force that moves us from one season to the next. In the same way that seeds need to break open so that new plants and trees may take root, we must allow our hearts to break open to experience a deepened and expanded life. Having the courage to experience these feelings without judging them, suppressing them, or holding on to them is how we participate with Mother Nature in our own transformation. It is therefore important in fall, as in every season, to follow the movement of our feelings. Then, by virtue of allowing ourselves to be fully immersed in fall, we will by the power of life itself be moved into winter.

Winter is the place out of which new life is born. To understand the season of winter, it is helpful to consider the metaphor of an oak tree. An acorn contains a future oak tree. The only way it can manifest is if the acorn drops to the ground, is covered up, and spends the winter in the dark, allowing the elements to break it open so the roots can grow down and the sprout can come up. If we could talk to the acorn in the midst of winter, it would probably say, "Something's gone wrong! It's cold. It's dark. I can't tell which way is up or down.

FIGURE 4.1
The Cycle of Seasons

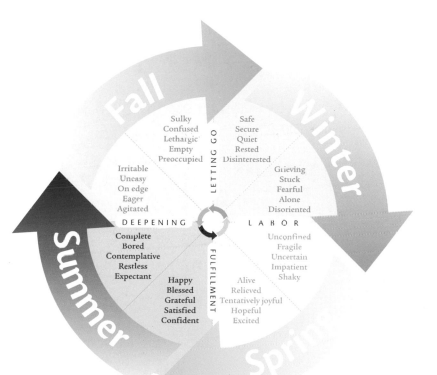

FIGURE 4.2

Emotions and the Cycle of Seasons

FALL	WINTER	SPRING	SUMMER
Irritable	Safe	Unconfined	Happy
Apprehensive	Tearful	Impulsive	Blessed
Unclear	Introspective	Tender	Passionate
Uneasy	Secure	Fragile	Grateful
Content	Quiet	Uncertain	Satisfied
Skeptical	Rested	Doubtful	Confident
Comfortable	Disinterested	Impatient	Delighted
Annoyed	Anxious	Shy	Festive
Restless	Defeated	Shaky	Elated
On edge	Powerless	Sensitive	Liberated
Eager	Resistant	Encouraged	Free and easy
Agitated	Angry	Interested	Fortunate
Hesitant	Threatened	Eager	Relaxed
Sulky	Grieving	Alive	Compassionate
Indecisive	Stuck	Relieved	Peaceful
Disappointed	Fearful	Passionate	Joyful
Disenchanted	Sad	Tentatively joyful	Complete
Frustrated	Heartbroken	Lucky	Bored
Confused	Humiliated	Hopeful	Contemplative
Ambiguous	Rejected	Amazed	Restless
Lethargic	Alone	Excited	Expectant
Empty	Paralyzed	Blessed	Understanding
Preoccupied	Depressed	Reassured	Tenacious
	Disoriented		

What is happening to me?" But it is precisely because of this breaking open that the acorn will experience its full potential.

We, too, must be willing to endure the darkness of winter and allow our hearts to break open even in the midst of disorientation, uncertainty, and sadness. We must let everything that no longer serves us fall away to realize our full potential as human beings capable of love and compassion. This releasing may involve losing a friend or partner, a job, or long-held beliefs. During the darkness of winter it is often difficult to sense movement, causing us to feel stuck or powerless, afraid of never seeing light again. Conditioned to avoid discomfort, we may want to run away from winter by eating, drinking, shopping, shutting down emotionally, or picking fights. And yet, in demonstrating the courage to stay present and gestate we ensure that the darkness of a personal winter prepares us for renewal and transformation, a lesson I learned from the grieving mother of a three-year-old.

My heart skipped a beat as I entered Anne's home. Over the fireplace hung a life-size photo of her daughter, Kaylee, at the beach, her eyes bright, smiling at a pail full of sand while holding a plastic shovel.

Anne was in the darkest part of her winter. She hadn't left the house in weeks. The rooms were gloomy and in need of cleaning. Wearing a necklace that held a sprinkling of her daughter's remains, Anne described her days as full of hopelessness, admitting she couldn't see a reason to live. Unable to cry, she wondered if she would ever feel alive again.

I promised her that with time and support she would find her way through her darkness. Later, as I prepared to leave, she agreed to go to the local support group, even though she didn't think it would help.

I was aware that the darkness of Anne's personal winter had scared her. And yet, I also noticed that she found comfort and safety in this dark night of the soul. Just as bears hibernate in winter, so it seemed important for her healing that she withdraw into her grief. I knew that nothing could be done to hasten her emergence from winter, that her cycle of seasons had to progress naturally.

As we continued to visit over several months, I saw that the circumstances of life that were breaking open Anne's heart had a direct connection to the immersion that would transform her. As difficult as it was for her to live from one day to the next, she eventually found the strength to transform her grief at losing a child into a willingness to help other children by doing housekeeping for a local children's hospital. It was through her deep commitment to feeling and expressing the pain of her broken heart that she gradually found meaning as she moved through the dark winter toward the light of spring.

Having the courage to stay present in the darkness of winter, allowing our hearts to break open, and experiencing feelings without rushing them or pushing them away, is how we cooperate in moving from winter into spring. It is the same way a mother cooperates with the process of labor while birthing her child.

Spring is the time of seeing light at the end of the tunnel, when hope begins to arise. We are often so happy to be emerging out of darkness that at first we only feel excited and relieved. But as we journey deeper into spring, we may feel fragile or uncertain. While such feelings can be unsettling, if we understand that they are simply a sign of moving deeper into spring we can experience them without pushing them away. If we could talk to an acorn that has just sprouted and broken through the ground, it might doubt the possibility of becoming a huge oak tree. Similarly, in spring we might feel uncertainty about who we are becoming or what will happen next.

I learned the signs of spring during a time when everything and everyone fell away because of a decision I had made to change the direction of my life. In following my own heart, I experienced such great pain that I wondered if it was even possible to recover. Then one day I felt a bit of happiness, although I only tentatively trusted it, questioning if it was okay to feel hope after all I had lost. My winter had been so long that seeing light at the end of the tunnel made me feel shaky and almost want to retreat to the safety of the dark. Now I know that these feelings—a combination of hope, uncertainty, and doubt—are typical of spring.

Despite any confusion we may have about feelings that emerge during this season, spring is a time of movement. It is when we begin to recognize that there may be life after the loss of a loved one, a relationship, a job, or a cherished belief—when we start feeling moments of happiness amidst our suffering, as I witnessed during a visit with a woman named Su Lin.

This particular day in the ICU I was asked if I could play my flute for a patient with an extreme headache. I walked into the darkened room to see a tiny woman lying in bed with a huge ice pack on her head. Back in a corner of the room were three people who appeared to be the patient's children. I usually ask who everyone is after introducing myself, but that day it didn't feel right. So I simply said, "Hi, I'm Julie, the hospital chaplain." No one moved or acknowledged my presence except the patient, who said, "Please come in. My name is Su Lin."

"Your nurse asked me to play my flute for you. I understand you have a bad headache," I replied.

"Yes, I do," she answered. "It would be lovely to hear your flute."

I instructed Su Lin to take a deep breath, close her eyes, and relax completely, simply allowing the bed to hold her up. Then I played my flute, the sounds filling the room with the music of American Indians and Celtics. When I finished, we sat in silence briefly, after which she said, in a lovely English-as-a-second-language accent, "I went deep into the mountain and then way down to the sea. It was so windy." I put my face up to hers to acknowledge the feelings she was expressing about her journey, and she squeezed my hand.

The simple act of playing the flute had connected us in a moment of meaning; we had become comrades deep inside the mountain and by the sea. As much as my flute music had touched her, she had touched me and allowed me a moment of full presence in a life that is often filled with striving, moving, and wanting.

We talked about allowing the depth of the mountain and the motion of the sea to clear the pain from her head. She took my hand and said, "Thank you."

I glanced at her family members sitting in the dark, each of them now smiling and nodding their appreciation.

In a brief moment, Su Lin had allowed a spark of light to penetrate her suffering and move her momentarily into spring. Sharing this moment of spring with Su Lin was an experience of joy.

Staying courageously present in the fragile state of spring, without retreating into darkness, invites the power of life to break us open to summer.

Summer is about completion, the subtle

process of becoming more comfortable, finding our authentic selves, and trusting the cycle of seasons, the life force, or God. In summer we feel confidence, peace, a sense of being in harmony and balance with the universe. Experiencing the contentment of summer comes as a direct result of being fully present in each of the preceding seasons, something I realized one Sunday at a nearby park.

On summer Sundays in California, people gather in parks to picnic with family and friends while listening to jazz or bluegrass bands—the perfect ending to a warm weekend. One such Sunday I watched a young barefoot couple in the distance jitterbugging to band music as their daughter toddled in circles around them. Suddenly, my four-year-old granddaughter chased after a dog she wanted to pet. I followed, making sure not to lose track of her in the crowd. When I caught up with her, I took her by the hand and headed back to our blanket on the grass.

"Julie, it's Bill and Sarah!" I heard someone call. I turned to see the couple I had been watching dance. Seeing them close up, I realized I had married them two years earlier in a particularly meaningful wedding because three years before that Sarah's six-month-old son, Michael, had died of a rare muscle disease. Sarah had divorced his father, wondering whether she would ever know happiness again.

Now, as she introduced me to her one-year-old daughter, Amanda, I saw her joy and pride at being a new mother. "Congratulations! She's adorable!" I swooned. "You look very happy."

"I am. I never thought I'd feel this way. I still carry Michael in my heart every day," Sarah admitted, "and now it is okay."

I watched as the threesome walked away, grateful to see the cycle of seasons expressed so beautifully through Sarah's transformation.

Summer is initially the season in which we all want to stay. Just as we want to run from winter, we want to remain in summer. But as we move deeper into summer, we may begin to feel a bit bored or restless. Such anticipation of a change on the horizon can be the beginning of movement from summer into fall, followed by another cycle of seasons.

By virtue of completing one cycle, we are moved into the next, with the ability to experience life more profoundly and expansively. Although people often struggle with the idea that they may be revisiting old feelings as they cycle once again through the seasons, with each new cycle it is important to remember the age-old saying "We never step in the same river twice." Every year, my Rose of Sharon goes through the same seasons as the year before but emerges a little taller and fuller.

In addition to repeatedly experiencing the cycle of seasons, it is important to understand that we can simultaneously be in different seasons in various areas of our lives, such as spring in our primary relationship, winter in our job, and fall in our health. We can also be in the same season in many areas of our lives. Regardless of which parts of our lives are in a particular season, it is important to trust the wisdom of the cycle.

We are affected not only by our own cycle of seasons but by the cycles of people close to us. For example, when a spouse or loved one suddenly wins the lottery, we may automatically be dropped into summer with its feelings of gratitude and elation. Or when someone we love dies, regardless of what season we have been in we almost always drop into winter. But even though our cycle of seasons may be affected by that of others, in trusting the cycle of seasons and allowing ourselves to remain present with our feelings, eventually our evolution through our own cycle progresses.

Interestingly, it doesn't always feel like we are moving forward through the seasons, especially when we seem to be moving back and forth between two seasons before moving definitively to the next. A wonderful example of this in nature is spring in Sacramento. Every year in February, Sacramentans experience two weeks of beautiful, warm weather, making it seem like spring has arrived, followed by a return of the windy and rainy weather characteristic of winter. I have come to understand that such shifting back and forth between the past season and the coming one is part of the transitional movement. Similarly, when transitioning between seasons in our lives we can be like a baby learning to walk, often taking tentative forward steps then backing up or falling down before moving more confidently to the next season.

Another good example of this phenomenon is the terminal agitation that people nearly always demonstrate when they are dying. Days or hours before death they may become restless, removing their clothes, pulling at the bedsheets, attempting to get out of bed, or speaking with people already dead. In this state, it seems as if the dying have an awareness of the need to let go, while simultaneously wanting to hang on to life.

A classic case of someone going back and forth between seasons before moving definitively forward occurred in an eighteen-year-old blind woman named Brianna, who was dying of a brain tumor. After being unconscious for several days, she suddenly bolted upright in bed, head turned toward the window, and said, "No, I am not coming yet." She was apparently having a conversation with someone on the other side, preparing to die but not yet ready.

Brianna did what we all do in life's transitions—talking about it and resisting it before eventually giving in to the power of our life cycle. Dying is really nothing more than allowing the cycle of seasons to propel us from one moment into the next, just as it does during all other transitions in our lives. As we come to trust the cycle of seasons in our daily experiences, we build a foundation for trusting it when faced with the dying of those we love or our own impending death.

CHAPTER FIVE

Trusting the Cycle of Seasons

Live in simple faith . . .
just as this trusting cherry
flowers, fades, and falls.

—Issa

*T*rusting the cycle of seasons enables us to live with less fear and anxiety. One of the biggest obstacles to trusting the personal cycle of seasons is our habit of judging things as good or bad. When we see emotions and circumstances in these terms, it is tempting to want to resist the natural progression of seasons. On the other hand, working with the dying has taught me to

stay open to the presence of good in all things, which became strikingly clear upon meeting Hope.

Even before she was born, Hope was diagnosed as terminal due to a genetic flaw. Born three weeks early, she became a hospice patient at five days of age. When I came to visit, Hope's mother, Jordan, answered the door, holding her newborn wrapped in a soft, white blanket, making it difficult at first to tell that anything was wrong with the baby.

"I can't believe this is happening," Jordan said. "Tony and I were so happy to be pregnant. It took us two years of fertility treatments and now this. I have fallen so completely in love with this baby. I've only had her for five days and I can't imagine my life without her," Jordan cried.

"Would you like to hold her?" she asked, offering the baby to me.

I took her and peered into the blanket. "How are you doing, little one?" I asked as if only she and I were in the room. "Welcome to the planet."

"Why do you think this is happening?" Jordan

questioned. "I wonder if I didn't take good enough care of myself during my pregnancy or if I'm being punished."

Jordan and I spent the afternoon talking about why a soul would come to the planet for such a short time and wondering what we were to learn from Hope.

The next two weeks would show us. Hope's days were filled with visits from her grandmother, her aunt, her hospice team, and neighbors. She ate occasionally, cried some, and slept most of the time. Everyone who came in contact with Hope was strongly and positively affected by her presence, as if there were no barriers between her and others. She broke open hearts just by showing up.

Hope's vulnerability gave us permission to stop defending our hearts. Not only did she share her journey with us, we shared our journeys with one another. By the time she died, we had become family—Hope's family. Hope died gracefully without a struggle, simply letting the cycle of seasons move her into the next moment.

Repeatedly living through transitions can teach us how to accept the struggles during the transition of dying. This seems to be the beauty and the challenge of life. Sometimes, however, the appearance of challenge makes it difficult to see that nothing has gone wrong. It was my journey with Betsy that taught me the cycle of life always knows what it is doing.

At midnight I picked up the phone, startled out of sleep while comfortably snuggled up to my new husband. "Julie," Alex said apologetically, "I'm so sorry, but can you talk to Betsy? I'm handing her the phone," he said.

"Julie, Alex is trying to kill me. He wants to sleep on the floor next to me, but I don't want him anywhere near me. I want someone to come and care for me but not him. Here, you talk to Alex and tell him to leave," Betsy demanded.

After Alex explained that his wife Betsy, facing death, had become paranoid and fitful, he added, "Our neighbor Sue is coming over, and I'll leave the room so Betsy can feel safe."

Hearing his breaking heart over the phone, I told Alex that some of this behavior was not uncommon.

Despite relative calm during the daytime, the nights had become nightmarish for Betsy and Alex. Each morning, Alex would greet me at the door heavy with grief at losing his kind, steady wife to what seemed like a demon. A man of few words and great depth, he would ask, "Why is this letting go so painful for her? She has trained so long and hard to have a peaceful death." His questions echoed my own. It appeared that Betsy, my dear friend of several years who had taught me much about the unseen part of life, had been forsaken in her moment of greatest need.

It wasn't until I stood in front of 350 people at Betsy's memorial service, hearing myself say, "Betsy did it all in her final three weeks of life" that I understood her behavior. She had spent her life exploring the frontiers of her own soul, quelling her anger and fear with the balm of spirituality. I had often wondered during our visits why she hadn't expressed anger or fear. One day when I visited her, she listened to a tirade about my life coming apart at the seams. After finishing, when I asked Betsy why she didn't ever get angry, she replied, "I think I got a little mad yesterday when Mom called and couldn't do anything except tell me about her troubles. I hung up and thought to myself, 'Doesn't she get that I'm dying?'" At this moment, Betsy seemed proud that she had identified her anger and expressed it. But that was the last time she ever mentioned feeling angry.

Betsy's spiritual tradition had taught her that doing anything to strengthen her identity as a person separate from others didn't serve her. In fact, about a year before she died, Betsy told me, "Someone from the American Cancer Society asked me to talk about living with cancer. But I couldn't tell if I was considering it because I wanted to be of service or because I wanted recognition for being a strong survivor, so I decided not to do it. I don't want to do anything that feeds my ego."

I spent two years with Betsy as she practiced

living and dying. "There really isn't any difference between living and dying," she would say. I listened as she explained all that she was learning from Tibetan Buddhists, and she listened to me talk about the importance of giving expression to feelings. We were each like a mama bird regurgitating all she had for her fledgling, and we were also the baby bird, taking in every morsel.

On the day Betsy died, Alex called and said, "She just died, Julie." I could hear both sadness and relief in his voice.

When I arrived, he took me to her room. Following the Buddhist tradition, Betsy had asked that her body remain untouched for seventy-two hours, allowing her spirit to fully depart.

Alex said, "I have been so heartbroken over her venom toward me. I just wanted to make it peaceful for her, and I couldn't. But yesterday when she turned soft, I knew she would be okay."

Less than twelve hours earlier I had stood next to her bed as Betsy held my face in her hands and told me about the beauty and love she saw surrounding all of us. Her eyes had become as soft as a pink sky at sunset. Alex stood next to her at the other side of the bed witnessing this exchange between us. We all were in awe of the resurrection of pure love out of the ashes of despair and surrender.

Betsy showed me the importance of staying in the present moment without judging the process of life, remaining vulnerable and allowing the cycle of seasons to move us into our dying. Through trusting the cycle of seasons, we find that in both pain and joy there is an underlying meaning to rotation through them all, making us more willing to experience all of life—even the messy parts. Author and poet Nancy Wood illuminates this idea eloquently in her poem "The Circles of Life":

> *You shall ask*
> *What good are dead leaves*
> *And I will tell you*
> *They nourish the sore earth.*

You shall ask
What reason there is for winter
And I will tell you
To bring about new leaves.

You shall ask
Why are the leaves so green
And I will tell you
Because they are rich with life.

You shall ask
Why must summer end
And I will tell you
So that the leaves can die.[1]

The cycle of seasons does not promise to be easy. It does, however, promise to transform us. Consciously experiencing previously hidden aspects of the cycle gives us a new wisdom from which to begin each day, letting us know that life in its wisdom is living us and that nothing has gone wrong.

CHAPTER SIX

The Gift of Feelings

Fear not—what is not real,
never was and never will be.
What is real
always was and cannot be destroyed.

—Bhagavad Gita

In our culture, the value and purpose of experiencing feelings is often undermined. Almost all religious traditions teach us that we are made in the image of the Creator, but in pointing out the ways we fall short of that ideal they tell us we should rise above our feelings. Consequently, most of us have learned to control and suppress our emotions. But this does not serve us. It is important to understand that in the cycle of seasons all

feelings are necessary and are neither good nor bad. Fully experiencing our feelings is what breaks open our hearts, allowing us to engage fully in life, healing our inner wounds, and helping us trust the cycle of seasons. From this perspective we can see feelings as a gift and the broken-open heart in service of a greater purpose.

Early in my life I mistakenly believed that my emotions defined my identity, and I judged their value. As a result, the feelings that I labeled "bad" I pushed away, while those I labeled "good" I held on to. Later, upon realizing that the feelings accompanying each season are simply part of the life force moving us from one season to the next, I became more willing to experience all feelings without judging them as positive or negative, appreciating their potential for healing us and connecting us to others. Not only does acknowledging the feelings of each season support personal growth but it often assists others in moving through their own cycle of seasons, as was revealed in my experience of the connection between Cecile and her dog, Scotty.

I was a little winded when I walked into Cecile's upstairs apartment in a downtown tenement. Antoinette, the young woman who answered the door, showed me to her great-grandmother's room. There I noticed Cecile's mixed breed terrier tucked into the covers of her bed. "This is Scotty," said Cecile, smiling. "I can't get out of bed anymore, so Scotty refuses to leave, too." It was easy to see his loyalty to Cecile.

Cecile and I spent time talking about death and God. She was a stoic, pragmatic woman who didn't want a big fuss made over her after her death, saying, "I know where I want my funeral. I've been a member of St. Mary's my whole life, and they have a team that puts together the funeral mass. Will you let them know I'm getting close? I want to make sure my family doesn't have to worry about it." I agreed.

Over the course of the next several weeks, I met all of Cecile's caregivers—her daughter, grand-daughter, great-granddaughter—a very close-knit group of quiet, stoic women. And it was true, while her family caregivers rotated, Scotty never voluntarily took a break. He was fed on the bed, next to his failing mistress, and only reluctantly allowed himself to be carried down the twenty-five steps to the front yard to go potty.

Early one morning, I received a call from Antoinette saying Cecile was dying. "Will you come?" she asked with uncertainty in her voice. By the time I arrived, all the women of the family had gathered in Cecile's living room, certain she would not want them to witness her death.

"Is it okay if I go in?" I asked. "I'd like to say good-bye." They nodded their approval.

As always, Scotty was on the bed, only he didn't lift his head or wag his tail to greet me, as he usually did. Sitting next to the bed, I said, "Hi, Cecile, it's Julie. I've come to say good-bye. How are you doing?"

"I'm glad you've come, Julie. I'm dying," she whispered, smiling slightly and then closing her eyes. Scotty and I sat perfectly still as we watched Cecile take her last few breaths. Antoinette, who had quietly come to the doorway, asked tentatively, "Is she gone?" I answered, "She is."

Moments later we all stood next to Cecile's bed in silence, waiting for the mortuary to come take her body.

"We've got to do something about Scotty," said Antoinette. "I don't think I can move him." Scotty laid perfectly still, burrowed into Cecile's body, his eyes closed.

I asked if they would like me to pick him up. They nodded their consent. I leaned over the bed, petted Scotty, and told him it was time to go. I slowly slid my hands under his chest and belly. He offered no resistance, but as I lifted him he laid his head on my shoulder and let out a mournful cry. In that moment Scotty's grief broke open the hearts of all of us in the room, and everyone wept. Finding her courage, Antoinette then took the dog. We could hear him cry all the way down the stairs. It was as if Scotty had offered up his own pain to help the family express theirs. This little dog had allowed his heart to break open and, as a result, made it safe for the rest of us to allow our hearts to break open and connect with one another.

There is opportunity in every season to experience through emotions the awakening power of life. When I contemplate moments in which my heart has broken open, it hasn't mattered if the catalyst was sorrow or joy. The vulnerability itself is a powerful tool for change that enables us to connect to the depth of human experience. Such times are a reminder of how important it is not to make pain synonymous with bad or pleasure synonymous with good. In terms of the cycle of seasons, this means not judging winter as negative and summer as positive. With such judgments we create suffering for ourselves.

When we stop judging experiences in terms of good or bad, pleasurable or painful, we learn to be present with all feelings and operate in sync with the natural flow of life. This requires a conscious decision to change our perspective and the use of energy in our lives. When I remember that winter involves the breaking open of the heart for the purpose of awakening and that the seat of the broken-open heart is also the seat of the authentic self, it is easier to trust its process rather than run from it, and thus allow for transformation. And when I remember that summer involves pleasurable feelings that are impermanent, it is easier to trust its process rather than hoping it will never change, and thus allow for transformation. The broken-open heart of winter feeds the new birth of spring, for pain and discomfort are the messengers of possibility. The joy and pleasure of summer feeds expansion and the planting of new ideas in fall.

The art of valuing emotions without judgment is something dying people can easily help us learn. No dying individual has ever said to me, "I wish I had worked more" or "I wish I had made more money" or "I wish I had bought more stuff." Many, however, have said, "I wish I had taken the time to mend my relationship with my daughter" or "I wish

I had enjoyed life more every day" or "I wish I'd taken more time to find my true calling or be helpful to others."

Awakening and becoming more present in our lives requires slowing down enough to get in touch with our inner selves and honor our personal cycle of seasons. This also assists us in sharing with others their personal cycle of seasons, as I discovered when my husband was facing open-heart surgery.

The night before emergency surgery for coronary heart disease, my husband Ross and I lay in his hospital bed together and talked about the metaphor of the broken-open heart and how, in the morning, he would actually have his physical heart broken open. Both of us felt that this was a transition in our lives but at the same time feared the surgery's potential implications. Facing the possibility of Ross's death together heightened our awareness of each other's feelings, and the experience of sharing our broken-open hearts created a deeper intimacy and honesty.

We held on to each other and expressed our gratitude for Western medicine, the relief at finally knowing what was wrong, and our trust that it could be repaired. "I know you're going to make it through this," I said quietly, "but if you don't, I want you to know I have experienced the love of my life in you. If I never love again, I will not feel like I missed anything. I know how much you love me, and that would carry me through the rest of my life."

Ross nodded and added, "I know how much you love me, and we have had a wonderful life together."

The next day Ross spent nine hours in surgery, after which I stepped cautiously into his room. The ventilator was on. The doctors had explained it was standard procedure, but the sight was painful.

"You made it," I whispered, relieved.

Ross opened his eyes in acknowledgment.

After several hours, the ventilator was removed. As the attendant gently pulled it out, Ross's eyes opened wide. He gagged and momentarily panicked before beginning to breathe on his own, gestures that reminded me of a baby being born. I wondered what Ross was being born into.

The next five days proved to be some of the most challenging of our lives because of complications. Doctors spent hours watching, diagnosing, and reassuring. Day and night I tried to comfort, understand, and stay present. I had difficulty leaving Ross's bedside for fear something might happen that would take him away from me. The only thing I did every day without fail to keep my sanity was walk three miles and pray—talking to God, the enlightened ones, and ancestors, expressing gratitude and hope.

One morning after my walk I went home, where my friends Jean and Michelle, were waiting. Concerned about Ross, I sank to the floor and wept. There was nothing to say, nothing to fix, just weeping to do. I realized in those few moments that Ross's heart surgery was not only about him being transformed through the breaking open of his heart, both physically and emotionally, but also about me being transformed through the breaking open of my heart, and a further transformation of us both by the power of life.

This experience has taught me the importance of sharing with others their personal cycle of life as a means of achieving intimacy with them. It has also impressed on me the significance of allowing *others* to support *me* so that I have the awareness of a helpful, loving presence in my life—something greater than myself. The challenge of remaining present and hopeful in the midst of a crisis has been a crucial test of my ability to trust the cycle of seasons.

We die how we live. Practicing being present in our living prepares us for being present to our dying. If we have practiced slowing down and permitting our hearts to break open during life, leading to awakening, we will know how to do it in dying. For the process of dying is simply allowing life to break us open into the next season of awakening.

CHAPTER SEVEN

Holding on and Holding Away

Be tough in the way a blade of grass is:
rooted, willing to learn,
and at peace with what is around it.

—Natalie Goldberg

Slowing down enough to feel our emotions and get in touch with our inner selves gives us the opportunity to notice what we are desperately trying to hold on to or are scared of and holding away. Buddhists tell us there are two things that create suffering: holding on and holding away.

Once we feel the suffering caused by our holding on or holding away, our hearts soften and we can empathize with the suffering of oth-

ers rather than judge them. With a softened heart, we can see that all people are doing the best they can, that each of us lives with pain, and each of us will die. A softened heart is the place of deep abiding joy that sustains us from the inside out, even in the midst of pain. It is this power of vulnerability that propels us through the cycle of seasons.

The cycle of seasons, in moving us from fall into winter, winter into spring, spring into summer, and summer into fall, shows us that everything is impermanent, and thus it is neither possible nor desirable to hold on to anything or any state of being as we must follow the movement of the cycle of life. If, in moments of pain, we can remember that the life force is moving us naturally through the seasons, and that all circumstances of life are impermanent, we can then choose to honor our vulnerability rather than holding on or holding away, as I learned from an eighty-six-year-old mother while her son lay dying.

Emily asked me to play my flute for her fifty-six-year-old husband, Jack, who was dying. "I think he's ready to die," she said, "but he's hanging on for some reason. All I can think of is that his mother, Iris, hasn't been able to say good-bye. For months I've asked her to do it, and she refuses."

I had also attempted to talk with Jack's mother several times over the past few months, and she had declined to say good-bye to Jack, assuring me he would be okay.

"Jack, it looks like you're getting ready to go," I said gently, stroking his cheek. He did not respond. I crawled onto the bed, sat cross-legged next to him, and began playing my flute. Iris was sitting in a rocker at the foot of the bed.

Jack had never wanted to talk about dying. He said he wanted to stay positive. I played my flute for him every time I visited, which usually brought tears to his eyes. This time I wondered if he could even hear me. He was so still, it was hard to tell that he was breathing. When I finished playing, there was a moment of silence.

Then, as if in a slow-motion film, without opening his eyes or saying a word Jack raised his arms and clapped three times. To me, it was as though Carnegie Hall had erupted into applause. Jack could no longer eat, turn himself over in bed, or talk, and yet somewhere in his heart he had found the strength to deliver his gift of joy and appreciation.

Iris was bent over in the rocker. I got on my knees to look into her face and asked, "Have you said good-bye?" Iris shook her head no, unable to speak through her tears.

"I think it's time," I encouraged her. "He needs you to say good-bye. It's okay to tell him you'll miss him. It's okay to let him know you will be all right, even though your heart is breaking."

"I've known for a while now that he was dying. I just couldn't bring myself to admit it," Iris said.

"What I know, Iris, is that you cannot get through this without your heart breaking. The hardest thing we do is say good-bye to the people we love. You brought Jack onto the planet. He may be waiting for you to let him go. Do you think you can say good-bye today?" I asked.

"You're right, my heart is breaking, but I know it's time," she admitted. "I will say good-bye today. But I need a few minutes alone with him."

Although I never knew what Iris said to Jack that day, when I saw her three months later she had a spark in her eye and was able to communicate with others again. Undoubtedly, the breaking open of Iris's heart through the loss of her son showed her the power of vulnerability to move her toward greater awakening and joy.

Once we become aware of how our holding on or holding away can cause ourselves or others suffering, we can learn to release judgment and better accept the natural rotation of the cycle of seasons, opening ourselves to greater freedom and joy. Repeatedly living through transitions teaches us the impermanence of everything and how to live without grasping or pushing anything away. When we understand that contrasting feelings are necessary expressions of the rotation through the cycle of seasons, we become more willing to experience all of life and are no longer invested in holding on to pleasure and holding away pain. The following poem by artist and musician Rashani Réa, entitled "The Unbroken," expresses how contrasting feelings are inextricably linked:

> *There is a brokenness*
> *out of which comes the unbroken,*
> *a shatteredness out of which blooms*
> *the unshatterable.*
> *There is a sorrow*
> *beyond all grief which leads to joy;*
> *and a fragility*
> *out of whose depths emerges strength...*
>
> *There is a hollow space*
> *Too vast for words*
> *Through which we pass with each loss,*
> *Out of whose darkness*
> *We are sanctioned into being.*

There is a cry deeper than all sound
whose serrated edges cut the heart
as we break open to the place inside
which is unbreakable and whole,
while learning to sing.[1]

In the same way that light follows darkness and joy follows sorrow, the seasons follow one another. It is important to embrace all our seasons and stop judging some experiences and feelings as good and others as bad. They are all simply parts of life in its wisdom.

Life knows what it is doing. It doesn't matter if our minds do not understand the process. What matters is that we stay present in it long enough to perceive the wisdom of life's natural movement through us. Life, in its wisdom, opens us to our true nature—that of loving, compassionate, joyful beings.

CHAPTER EIGHT

Letting Go

Fill my heart with Love,
that my every teardrop
may become a star.

—Hazrat Inayat Kahn

In the West, we spend our time and energy on prolonging life, often to the point of denying death. We are preoccupied with the body, physical comfort, and happiness. We allow ourselves to judge one another by what we have, and in so doing lose sight of our connectedness. Asleep to the reality of our temporary status as residents of earth, we forget that one day we will have to let it all go.

If we want to make a positive impact in our world, we must become willing to change our perspective on life and death. When we embrace the fact that death is the great equalizer, seeing ourselves and others as human beings who are going to die, it is easier to be honest and compassionate. When we are willing to look past circumstances and recognize that people are doing their best, our defensiveness fades and we can be curious, helpful, and understanding. To gain such a perspective, we must first become willing to cease judging circumstances as good or bad, right and wrong, and trust the inherent cycle of seasons. Then we must choose to stay present with the feelings of each season, which keeps us vulnerable, with our hearts undefended. When we allow ourselves to be vulnerable, we create a safe place for others to share their vulnerability with us. This place of vulnerability is actually the seat of authentic power that frees us from suffering and is a tool for change.

We can remain willing to allow our hearts to break open and experience the feelings of all seasons by considering that there is a power for good in the universe that is always present and that the breaking open of the heart resulting in transformation starts at birth. Our initial experience of birth is one of a broken-open heart and vulnerability leading to change and growth. Newborns are so open that they simply surrender to the power of life. We often comment on how close to God newborns seem, perhaps because they so willingly surrender to the cycle of seasons.

As we grow from infancy to childhood and childhood to adulthood, we can become increasingly distrustful of the cycle of seasons due to social or ideological conditioning and fear of death. When we begin to experience the physical decline that comes with aging, we often stop trusting the cycle and act as though something's gone wrong. Making an enemy of our natural life process, including our death, however, causes unnecessary suffering.

In truth, dying often has little to do with the body. I have seen people who appear relatively healthy die unexpectedly, and I have seen others who struggle for each breath live months beyond all predictions. Consequently, I have come to believe that dying is really just another transformation in which we actively participate through the power of our broken-open hearts, an understanding I developed while inadvertently setting aside my own agenda and following the wisdom of another's soul.

One day Dena, a hospice nurse, announced, "We have a new patient, Margaret, who wants to see you. I told her you play the Native American flute. She wants to hear it, but she doesn't want to talk." I wondered how I was going to do that as I always talked with my patients, but I agreed.

When I arrived, Margaret was sitting in an overstuffed rocking chair in the living room. I greeted her, saying, "Hi, Margaret, I understand you want to hear me play the flute." She nodded. Seated on an ottoman in front of her, I played for several minutes with my eyes closed, then opened them to catch Margaret attempting to conceal her tears. I continued to play, even though I wanted to stop and ask what she was feeling.

When finally I put the flute down and took Margaret's hand, without looking at me, she said, "I admire anyone who can make music. I can't, but I just love it."

Every week for six weeks we did the same thing: I played my flute, Margaret cried, I held her hand briefly, then said good-bye and left. There was only one change during those six weeks. After my third visit, Margaret allowed me to hug her before I walked out the door.

Then one afternoon I decided to drop in to see her on my way home. We'd grown very fond of each other, and I wanted to surprise her. When I arrived, she was in bed and said, "Help me sit up." During the next hour, Margaret told me her life story, describing her childhood, her career, her marriage to the love of her life, the struggles and the delights of raising her children, her fears, her heartaches, and her hopes. She then told me how much she appreciated our visits and how much the flute music touched her.

Realizing her story was finished, I helped her lay back on the bed. "Will you play the flute for me?" she asked. I played. She cried. We shared a hug. Then she said, "I love you."

With a kiss on her cheek, I answered, "I love you, too."

The next morning there was a message at the office telling me Margaret had died during the night. I was surprised, as she hadn't appeared to be dying when I left. But I realized that the timing and manner of her death had been perfect. She had died the way she wanted, with silence and with music. She had gotten in touch with her feelings and died when she was ready. For her, quiet and music created trust. Trust established a safe place to tell her story. Telling her story generated release, and release allowed the beginning of a new story—transformation through death.

If dying is not about the body, it follows that life is not about the body. The body is simply the vehicle through which we live, love, awaken, and allow the cycle of seasons to expand us into greater experience, as my beloved canine of thirteen years helped me see.

I sat on the floor next to Sadie, my big Bernese mountain and retriever mix, telling her if she wanted to die on her own it was okay, but if she needed help, I'd help. She had won my heart when I found her at a shelter wanting to get to the tennis ball lodged in the concrete drainage ditch at the end of the kennel. My father had just died, and it was clear from our first glance that we needed each other.

I thought of Sadie as my guide dog. Over the years, it had often seemed that she knew me better than I knew myself. She had always been with me providing comfort, love, playfulness, or loyalty, depending on what the moment called for. Now it was painful for her to walk and her spark was beginning to fade.

After work some days later, I found Sadie lying with foggy eyes next to my bed, where I had left her that morning. Her message was as clear to me as if she had said it out loud—that she was ready to die. I was committed to my promise of helping her and made an appointment with the veterinarian for the next day. That night Sadie and I slept together as usual, only this time we slept on the floor. She didn't have enough energy to get on the bed, and I didn't have enough strength to lift her. She raised her head occasionally to acknowledge my breaking heart and then drifted back to sleep. I ran my hand over her peaceful face and gentle body, saying good-bye.

The next morning, a friend and I carried Sadie from the car into the veterinarian's exam room. Dr. Susan examined her and confirmed that it was time for Sadie to go. As Dr. Susan got down on the floor, she began to cry and explained that her two-year-old retriever had died suddenly three days ago. She whispered into Sadie's ear, "Please say hi to Sammy for me." Sadie raised her head, as if in response to the request.

I fed her treats as Dr. Susan slipped the needle into Sadie's back leg. Seconds later, her head dropped. I was struck by the absence of Sadie's life force from her body, making her no longer even look like my dog. I understood in a moment of clarity that her body was simply the vehicle through which she had expressed her loving spirit. I am grateful to have witnessed the grace with which she died and the clarity with which she taught me the truth about the body being only a temporary house for the spirit.

This experience helped me realize that we may be looking at dying backwards. We have come to believe that when the body gets ill or damaged it's time for the life force to leave. Perhaps we should consider that, in reality, the life force—the innate wisdom within us—knows when it is time to move on, and it is then that the body becomes injured or ill. This theory, which might better explain the unpredictability of death, was driven home to me by the sight of a comatose teenager in the ICU.

"Julie, I need your help," the ICU doctor said as I answered the phone. "I have to talk with the family of a teenager who was beaten unconscious by a gang of boys yesterday and is on life support."

I stopped to see nineteen-year-old Amid before going to the meeting, feeling pain as I looked at him and cringing at the thought of what it must be like for parents to see a once-vibrant son on a ventilator. I didn't know how I could help his parents decide what to do next.

Amid had come to the United States just two years earlier to live with his father in the land of the free and realize his dreams. Now divorced, his parents were facing turning off life support and allowing him to die.

Anger flared and tears fell as this couple, their hearts broken open, attempted to make the best decision for their son. In the end, they opted to continue life support, agreeing to trust their God's plan that when it was time their son would either awaken or die.

This experience underscored, for me, the unpredictability of death and the fact that it seems based more on the personal evolution of the life cycle and less on one's age, health, or other prospects. Such unpredictability can undermine our trust in the wisdom of the life cycle. When life doesn't go according to our plan and we are suddenly faced with challenges we could not have anticipated, believing that something has gone wrong, it can be helpful to look at life the way it really happens, not how we think it should happen. Life is a mystery, which means that sometimes it will not go according to our plan. Living in a mystery means that sometimes children die before their parents. Living in a mystery means that sometimes loved ones take their own lives. Living in a mystery, it is important to stay open, keep asking questions, and live consciously in the present moment, fully engaged no matter what the circumstances.

The struggle we often face in living life consciously and fully is in accepting losses and difficulties. At such times, it is important to remember that losses and difficulties are not a means of punishing us. Life is not about particular forms of difficulties, whether they involve physical illness, mental illness, addiction, abuse, or loss. It is about whether we will allow the circumstances of our lives to break open our hearts so we fully experience emotions and empathetically connect with others. The path to true peace of mind may be in letting life break open our hearts, whether in joy or in sorrow, giving us the opportunity to be transformed.

Thus even while facing loss or difficulty, we can remember that the darkness of winter is necessary for the breaking open of the heart. And we can have faith that everything in our lives helps us awaken to the truth of who we are.

Embracing the broken-open heart and allowing our losses and difficulties to assist us in better understanding who we are, rather than diminishing us, can help us expand and deepen our life experience. Trusting our cycle of seasons, regardless of the circumstances, allows us to build faith in something greater than ourselves. Acknowledging that there is a power for good in the cycle of seasons—the cycle of life—offers us a new paradigm from which to live.

CHAPTER NINE

Awakening

May all things move and be moved in me
and know and be known in me.
May all creation
dance for joy within me.

—Chinook Psalter

Life often has an agenda different from our own. Some unexpected events bring joy and others pain, both of which are part of the life cycle. When unexpected events bring joy—such as new love or landing the perfect job—we trust life and feel as if everything is right with the universe. When unexpected events bring pain—such as losing a job or the death of a loved one—we distrust life and feel as if we are being treated unfairly.

Other times, situations that we at first judge as promising can become troublesome. For example, after the first blush of falling in love a relationship can become more challenging, requiring us to learn true intimacy and trust by undefending our hearts and increasing our capacity for compassion. But even circumstances that cause pain and difficulty keep us awakening to the wisdom of life, the cycle of seasons moving in perfect timing and rhythm.

Many times I hear people later express gratitude for situations that resulted in a broken-open heart, explaining they wouldn't have chosen their heartbreaking experience but in retrospect recognize it as a gift. It is very beneficial to maintaining a positive perspective on life if we can believe that no matter where we are at any given time, whether in a trusting or painful state of being, we are in the sacred cycle of life, awakening ever more deeply to the truth of who we are, as I found out from a newly widowed thirty-six-year-old mother.

I met Michelle on the California coast when she and a friend approached me saying they had attended a workshop I had just completed on the cycle of life. Hilda, Michelle's friend, was a vivacious woman in her fifties, and Michelle appeared to be about thirty. "Michelle's husband just died," Hilda announced. "That's why we came to your workshop."

Because of Michelle's age, I thought perhaps I had heard wrong, so I asked, "How long ago did he die?"

"Three months ago," Michelle admitted, a bit tentatively. She was clearly a woman who kept her feelings to herself.

Hilda invited me to join them for dinner that evening, and I gladly accepted. Over dessert, Michelle told me the story of how her husband, Kahl, had died. He had decided to enlist with the Air Force Reserves, and she had supported him in his decision, even though her heart had been broken at not being consulted in advance. She knew she and Keegan, their six-year-old son, would have to get used to Kahl being gone a lot.

"I couldn't imagine Kahl in the Air Force," Michelle reminisced. "I have always been a strong peace advocate and here was Kahl joining the military! When Kahl was deployed to Iraq, all my fears of him being injured or killed became real."

Michelle told me how her heart would sink every time the phone rang, afraid it could be a call from Kahl's commander with bad news. She also recounted the many phone conversations between her and Kahl. "After the first couple calls, we told each other 'I love you,' at the beginning because we never knew when the connection would get cut off," Michelle explained.

"Did Kahl die in Iraq?" I asked.

"No," Michelle replied. "He died after that. While in Iraq, he had gone beyond the call of duty by agreeing to take part in a risky mission. Because of that, upon returning to the States his name was put into a hat for a drawing to determine who would get to fly in an F-16. He won and was as excited as a child at Christmas. Though a little anxious, I was happy that his lifelong dream was coming true and at the same time my dream was coming true—that with this flight Kahl's commitment to the Air Force Reserves would be complete and he would come home for good.

"No one really knows for sure what happened," Michelle continued, wincing at the memory of her husband's death. "His commander phoned with news of his condition and urged me to fly to Miami as soon as possible.

"'Mrs. Walker, the information I have is that Sergeant Walker stopped breathing in flight, and as soon as the pilot realized there was a problem he turned the aircraft around. The ground team did CPR on him for fifty minutes until the airlift crew arrived and took over, but they aren't sure he's going to make it through the night,' he said.

"Keegan and I, along with Kahl's family, arrived in Florida to find Kahl unconscious and on life support. He appeared peaceful and asleep," she explained.

"Several days later we decided to remove life support. I was the last person to stand alongside him as his body gave in late that night. As I kissed him, my knees gave way and I crumpled to the floor. I have no memory of how long I lay there or of how I got back to the hotel. What I do remember is looking at Keegan, still sound asleep as the sun rose, and wondering, 'How am I going to tell him?'

"When Keegan awoke late the next morning, I hugged him and said, 'Hey, buddy, we have to talk.'

"He said, 'I know. Dad died. He came and told me he had to go now. That's why I slept late. I didn't want to stop dreaming about him.'

"My heart ached at the thought of Kahl making sure Keegan had a gentle experience of his dying while at the same time wanting to scream at the reality of my life.

"Ironically, one month later my father died from cancer, after telling us just a week earlier that he had been keeping his diagnosis a secret. It seemed unreal that four weeks after we turned off life support to Kahl I was standing at my father's bedside watching machinery breathe for him. I am grateful, though, that Dad could briefly communicate with me before he died. He even apologized for leaving at such a difficult time in my life. He wasn't concerned about dying but about me. Sometimes I just feel like I'm the one who's dead," Michelle confessed.

As she finished her story, I wondered what I could say to this young woman who was standing in the midst of what sounded like hell. I had just done a ninety-minute workshop explaining the cycle of life to illustrate that we are always awakening, in times of despair and pain as well as in times of exhilaration and joy, but looking at this beautiful, young, numb woman made me wonder if everything I proclaimed was just a construct in my own mind to help me face the pain of life.

Only later, after Michelle had taken a two-year end-of-life training with me, did I see that even in her circumstances life's wisdom was evident. During the training, Michelle faced her broken-open heart repeatedly and allowed herself to be transformed by the power of her vulnerability and grief. In response to an essay question asking my students about their personal experience with the broken-open heart, Michelle described it this way:

> From the first moment Kahl came home announcing he had enlisted in the Air Force Reserves, life has been doing what it does best—changing, changing me. Living in the middle of my broken-open heart has allowed me to trust in something much bigger than myself. Today I am content with standing in a new life, even though I don't know what that new life will bring.
>
> I still have moments of intense pain. I continue to experience a deep sense of loss that often takes me by surprise. At times my experience of grief has seemed an eternity, but as I practice living from the broken-open heart my life continues to expand. I have moments of sadness, fear, and anger, followed by days of joy, anticipation, and hope. I used to think I was crazy. Now I know this is life—life doing what life does, creating and expanding in every moment. I'm learning to trust life.

The greatest gift I have received through living from my broken-open heart is the deep awareness of how fragile life is. It is worth every effort to make sure I live from a place of love and compassion, and to make today count. After all, it might be the only day I get.

Through writing these words, Michelle revealed her willingness to fully participate in the messy, unpredictable nature of life. She also demonstrated her understanding that, despite circumstances involving pain or death, it was possible to awaken to new levels of courage, creativity, and trust in the cycle of seasons.

Some days I begin my daily walk with my dogs before sunrise and try to be conscious of precisely the moment when it turns from dark to light, but it is always difficult to pinpoint. I am aware of darkness, just a little brightening, and then it is light. In such times of reflection, it is clear to me that this is how the cycle of seasons works. We are aware of the darkness and pain, and then at some point we are aware of the light or relief without being able to determine exactly when the shift occurred. Yet even though we cannot always pinpoint the shifts, or stop resisting their impact on us, the cycle of seasons is continually moving us into expanded awareness and love.

Always we are at liberty to awaken further and cooperate with the wisdom of life. When we do cooperate, embracing life, even its messy and painful parts, we are transformed. We are then able to see that as some things fall away—such as people, pets, ideals, beliefs, and fears—other things take up residence in the empty places left behind, like a new love, friendships, or perceptions that will become part of a deepened experience of life. And the more we feel the messy, wonderful, horrible, fantastic, loving nature of who we are, the closer we come to living a full-tilt unapologetic life. Ultimately, while walking through transitions consciously, we come to see that we are constantly awakening and that each new dawn brings with it a deepening trust and willingness to step into the life-changing power of the broken-open heart.

Notes

Chapter 4

1. Thich Nhat Hanh, *No Death, No Fear* (New York: Penguin, 2002), 40.

Chapter 5

1. Nancy Wood, "The Circles of Life," *Many Winters* (New York: Doubleday Books for Young Readers, 1974). Reprinted by permission of the author.

Chapter 7

1. Rashani Réa, "The Unbroken," *Beyond Brokenness* (Bloomington, IN: Xlibris, 2009). Reprinted by permission of the author.

Selected Reading

Chödrön, Pema. *The Places That Scare You*. Boston: Shambhala Publications, 2001.

Hanh, Thich Nhat. *No Death, No Fear*. New York: Penguin, 2002.

Kuebelbeck, Julie. *Caregiver Therapy*. St. Meinrad, IN: Abby Press, 1995.

Levine, Stephen. *A Year to Live*. New York: Bell Tower, 1997.

Mountain Dreamer, Oriah. *The Invitation*. New York: HarperCollins, 1999.

Muller, Wayne. *Sabbath*. New York: Bantam Press, 1999.

Rinpoche, Sogyal. *Tibetan Book of Living and Dying*. New York: HarperCollins, 2002.

Stillwater, Michael. *Graceful Passages*. Novato, CA: New World Library, 2003.

About the Author

Julie Interrante, MA, has her master of arts degree in Consciousness Studies from the Holmes Institute in Los Angeles, California. She is the senior minister of the Albuquerque Center for Spiritual Living and founder of the Compassionate Arts Project, through which she teaches the art of compassion. She has more than twenty years of experience serving as chaplain in both acute care and home hospice care settings.

Julie is a contributing author to *What Helps the Most When You Lose Someone You Love* and coauthor of *Caregiver Therapy*, both published by Abbey Press. A gifted speaker and teacher, she brings humor, compassion, and a deep respect for life to all that she does. A playful grandmother, she makes her home in New Mexico with her husband, Ross, and their two dogs, Daisy and Maggie.

ORDER FORM

Quantity   **Amount**

_____ *The Power of a Broken-Open Heart: Life-*
      Affirming Wisdom from the Dying ($15.00) _____

Sales tax of 6.75% for New Mexico residents _____

Shipping and handling ($3.00 for first book;
      $1.50 for each additional book) _____

Total amount enclosed _____

Quantity discounts available

Method of payment:

☐ Check or money order enclosed (made payable to
      Compassionate Arts Publishing in US funds only)

☐ MasterCard ☐ VISA ☐ Discover   Exp._____/_____

Credit Card # _____

Ship to (please print):

NAME _____

ADDRESS _____

CITY/STATE/ZIP _____

PHONE _____

Compassionate Arts
P U B L I S H I N G
PO Box 35466, Albuquerque, NM 87176
505-967-6865
www.compassionateartspublishing.com